초등영어 읽기독립

리딩 스타터 1
Reading Starter

3 단계

재능많은
영어연구소
지음

휴먼
어린이

초등영어 읽기독립 3단계
"28일만 따라 하면 술술 긴 글이 읽혀요!"

리딩 스타터 1 구성

 균형적 문해 접근법의 영어 읽기

여러분은 알파벳과 소릿값을 익히고 모음 파닉스를 배워 단어 읽기를 끝낸 후 사이트 워드로 문장 읽기까지 완료했어요. 여기서 나아가 모든 읽기 활동이 의미 있는 것이 되려면 균형적 문해 학습을 해야 해요.

리딩 스타터는 글자와 단어를 읽는 것을 넘어 진정한 읽기의 목적인 글을 읽고 이해하는 단계로 단어와 문장의 사전 지식을 익히고, 그 배경지식을 바탕으로 글의 내용을 이해하고 재확인하는 과정을 가져요.

2 **〈읽기 전 - 읽기 중 - 읽기 후〉의 3단계 읽기**

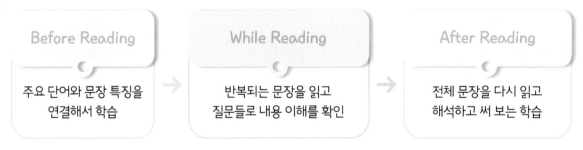

Before Reading		While Reading		After Reading
주요 단어와 문장 특징을 연결해서 학습	→	반복되는 문장을 읽고 질문들로 내용 이해를 확인	→	전체 문장을 다시 읽고 해석하고 써 보는 학습

리딩 스타터는 반복되는 문장 패턴을 이용해 그 안의 단어들을 바꿔 새롭게 만들어진 표현들을 담아 글을 구성했어요.
패턴을 이용한 간단한 글이지만 영어로 된 긴 글도 읽을 수 있다는 자신감을 갖게 하는 동시에 반복적이고 다양한 표현들을 통해 단어와 문장의 특징을 자연스럽게 익힐 수 있어요.

또한 초등생이 쉽게 접하는 일상생활의 표현들과 교과 과정에서 배우는 주제 중심 활동을 담은 내용들로 구성되어 쉽게 문장을 이해할 수 있으며, 친숙한 표현들을 통해 영어 읽기에 재미와 흥미를 불러일으켜요.

이렇게 만들었어요!

3 매일매일 읽기 독립! 자연스럽게 이루어지는 학습 계획

부담 없는 하루 학습량과 명확하고 목표에 맞는 학습 계획으로 읽기의 성장을 바로바로 확인할 수 있어요. 두 개의 유닛을 끝내고 나면 리뷰와 딕테이션(받아쓰기)을 하며 복습할 수 있어요.

Unit	Grammar	Sentence Pattern
01	a + 명사	I am a girl.
02	an + 명사	Is it an umbrella?
Unit 01~02 Review / Dictation		
03	in + (the) 장소	I am in the moon.
04	형용사 (크기/상태/특징/색깔)	It is small.
Unit 03~04 Review / Dictation		
05	명사s	I like cucumbers.
06	명사 + y	It is rainy.
Unit 05~06 Review / Dictation		
07	There are + 짝을 이루는 것	There are shoes.
08	불규칙한 복수 명사	Children love bears.
Unit 07~08 Review / Dictation		
09	주어 + 주요 동사	We play together.
10	주어에 따른 동사형 1	Matt likes sports.
Unit 09~10 Review / Dictation		
11	주어에 따른 동사형 2	She cries all day long.
12	부정문 1	I do not have breakfast.
Unit 11~12 Review / Dictation		
13	부정문 2	He does not work.
14	의문문	Do trees grow new leaves?
Unit 13~14 Review / Dictation		

• 《리딩 스타터》 1, 2권에서 각각 14가지 Grammar와 Sentence Pattern을 배울 수 있어요.

초등영어 읽기독립 3단계

리딩 스타터 1 특징

QR코드를 찍으면 오늘 배울 내용을
원어민의 정확한 발음으로 들을 수 있어요!

1 단어 / 문장 미리 보기

글을 읽기 전에 주요 단어와 문장을 미리 보고
글의 내용을 추측해 보며 단어와 문장을 연습해 봐요.

반복되는 문장과 그 문장의 특징을
살펴보고 따라 쓰며 익혀요.

2 본문 읽기

재미있는 일상생활이나 논픽션 등의 주제글을 읽고 글을 이해하는 법을 배워요.

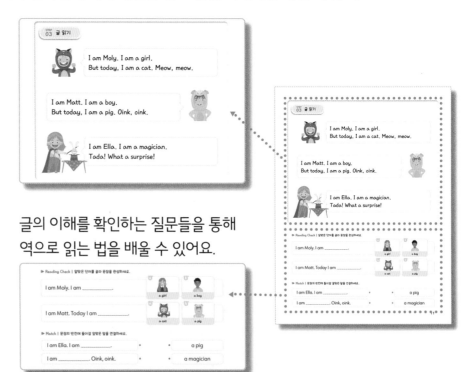

글의 이해를 확인하는 질문들을 통해
역으로 읽는 법을 배울 수 있어요.

3 한 문장씩 연습하기

배운 기초 단어들과 반복되는 문장으로 이루어진 글을 다시 읽고 전체를 다시 써 보기, 문장 완성하는 연습 등으로 글 읽기에 자신감을 채워 보세요.

반복되는 문장을 다시 쓰다 보면
자연스럽게 문장과 글을 재확인할 수 있어요.

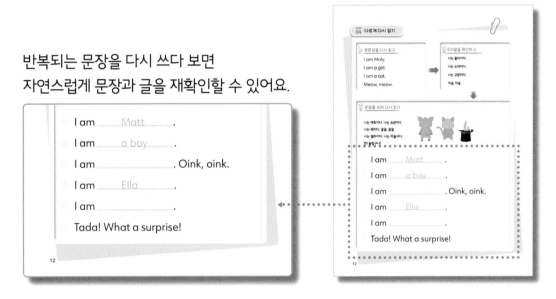

4 리뷰 및 딕테이션

이틀 동안 공부한 두 개의 유닛을 누적 반복하는 연습을 통해 빠르고 정확하게 읽을 수 있어요. 그리고 전체 글을 들으며 딕테이션(받아쓰기)을 할 수 있어요.

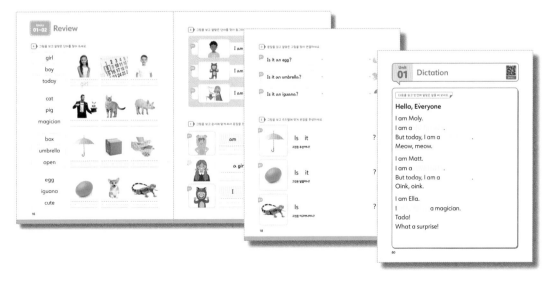

초등영어
3단계만 따라 하면
읽기독립이 된다!

하루 15분

1단계	2단계	3단계
단어 읽기	문장 읽기	긴 글 읽기
파닉스 1, 2	사이트 워드	리딩 스타터 1, 2

1단계 　파닉스 1, 2

40일만 따라 하면 단어가 읽힌다.

단어 읽기

파닉스 규칙 1
알파벳

파닉스 규칙 2
모음

파닉스로
낱글자에서 단어 읽기까지!
파닉스 떼기

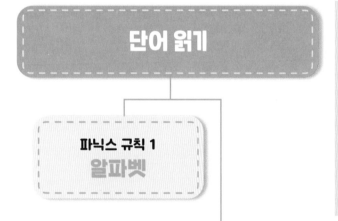

파닉스: 알파벳

글자 인지

음가 구별

글자 읽기

1단계 파닉스 알파벳으로 글자 읽기!

파닉스: 모음

단/장모음

이중 모음

단어 읽기

1단계 파닉스 모음으로 단어 읽기!

2단계 ▸ 사이트 워드

30일만 따라 하면 문장이 읽힌다.

문장 읽기

사이트 워드
단어 뜻과 활용

| 사이트 워드 |
| 단어 활용 |
| 초등 표현 |
| 문장 읽기 |

2단계 사이트 워드로 문장 읽기!

사이트 워드로 문장 읽기!

사이트 워드 120개, 초등 필수 문장 180개 학습

3단계 ▸ 리딩 스타터 1, 2

28일만 따라 하면 긴 글이 읽힌다.

긴 글 읽기

읽기 첫 독립 1
기능어

읽기 첫 독립 2
문장 규칙

**문장 규칙으로
혼자 읽기까지!**

초등 3, 4학년 필수 영단어와 문장 규칙 학습

| 주제 단어 |
| 기능어 |
| 문장 규칙 |
| 단락 읽기 |

3단계 기능어로 첫 읽기 도전!

| 주제 단어 |
| 문장 규칙 |
| 문장별 확인 |
| 단락 이해하기 |

3단계 문장 규칙으로 첫 읽기 도전!

Part 1

Unit 01

_____ 월 _____ 일

나의 평가는?
☆☆☆☆☆

Hello, Everyone

• Unit 01을 끝내고 p.80 Dictation을 하세요.

Unit 02

_____ 월 _____ 일

나의 평가는?
☆☆☆☆☆

Happy Birthday

• Unit 02를 끝내고 p.81 Dictation을 하세요.
• Review를 통해 Unit 01~02를 정리하세요.

Hello, Everyone

QR코드

STEP 01 기초 단어 익히기

소녀
girl

고양이
cat

오늘
today

소년
boy

돼지
pig

마술사
magician

STEP 02 기초 문장 익히기

사람이나 사물을 가리키는 명사일 때 〈a + 명사〉로 써요.

	명사	a + 명사
소녀 ➡	girl	I am a girl.
소년 ➡	boy	I am a boy.
고양이 ➡	cat	It is _____.

I am Moly. I am a girl.
But today, I am a cat. Meow, meow.

I am Matt. I am a boy.
But today, I am a pig. Oink, oink.

I am Ella. I am a magician.
Tada! What a surprise!

▶ **Reading Check** | 알맞은 단어를 골라 문장을 완성하세요.

I am Moly. I am _____.

a	b
a girl	a boy

I am Matt. Today I am _____.

a	b
a cat	a pig

▶ **Match** | 문장의 빈칸에 들어갈 알맞은 말을 연결하세요.

I am Ella. I am _____. •   • a pig

I am _____. Oink, oink. •   • a magician

영문장을 다시 읽고

I am Moly.
I am a girl.
I am a cat.
Meow, meow.

 우리말을 확인하고

나는 몰리이다.

나는 소녀이다.

나는 고양이다.

야옹, 야옹.

 문장을 쓰며 다시 읽기

나는 매트이다. 나는 **소년**이다.
나는 **돼지**다. 꿀꿀, 꿀꿀.
나는 엘라이다. 나는 **마술사**다.
짠! 놀랍구나!

→ I am _____Matt_____ .

→ I am _____a boy_____ .

→ I am _____. Oink, oink.

→ I am _____Ella_____ .

→ I am _____ .

→ Tada! What a surprise!

STEP 01 기초 단어 익히기

상자

box

열다

open

우산

umbrella

달걀

egg

이구아나

iguana

귀여운

cute

STEP 02 기초 문장 익히기

명사가 모음(a, e, i, o, u) 발음으로 시작할 때 〈an + 명사〉로 써요.

	명사	a + 명사
우산	umbrella	Is it an umbrella?
이구아나	iguana	Is it an iguana?
달걀	egg	Is it _____?

What is it?

Guess what is inside the box.

Is it an umbrella?

No, it isn't.

Is it an egg?

No, it isn't.

Is it an iguana?

No, it isn't. Open it.

Wow, it is a cute dog.

Happy birthday. It is for you.

*It isn't는 It is not의 줄임 표현이에요.

▶ **Reading Check** | 알맞은 단어를 골라 문장을 완성하세요.

It is about a birthday _____.

a box	b present

Is it an _____?

a egg	b dog

▶ **Match** | 문장의 빈칸에 들어갈 알맞은 말을 연결하세요.

A _____ is in the box.   •   •   umbrella

Is an _____ in the box?   •   •   dog

✌️ 영문장을 다시 읽고

Guess what is inside the box.
Is it an umbrella?
No, it isn't.
Is it an egg?
No, it isn't.

✌️ 우리말을 확인하고

상자 안에 무엇이 있는지 맞혀 봐.
그것은 우산이니?
아니, 그렇지 않아.
그것은 달걀이니?
아니, 그렇지 않아.

✌️ 문장을 쓰며 다시 읽기

상자 안에 무엇이 있는지 맞혀 봐.
그것은 이구아나이니?
아니, 그렇지 않아. 열어 봐.
와, 그것은 귀여운 개로구나.
생일 축하해. 그것은 너를 위한 거야.

→ ___Guess___ what is inside the box.

→ Is it _____?

→ No, _____ . Open it.

→ Wow, it is _____ .

→ Happy Birthday. _It is_ for you.

A 그림을 보고 알맞은 단어를 찾아 쓰세요.

girl
boy
today

girl

cat
pig
magician

box
umbrella
open

egg
iguana
cute

그림을 보고 알맞은 단어를 찾아 동그라미 하세요.

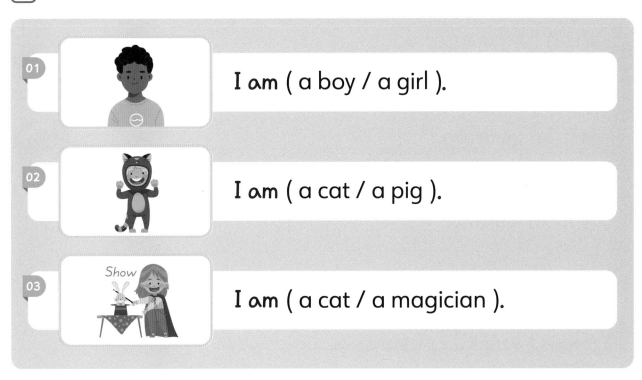

01 I am (a boy / a girl).

02 I am (a cat / a pig).

03 I am (a cat / a magician).

C 그림을 보고 순서에 맞게 써서 문장을 완성하세요.

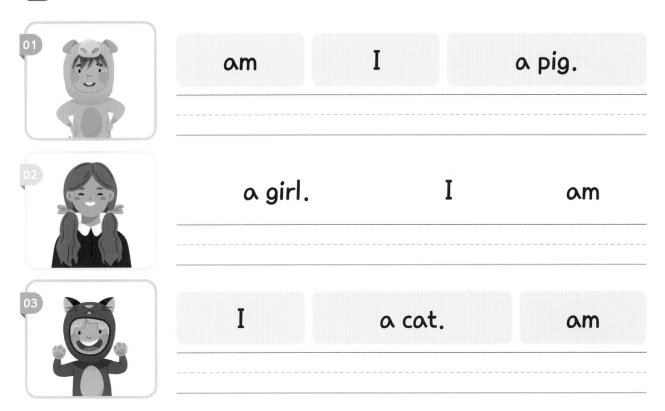

01 am   I   a pig.

02 a girl.   I   am

03 I   a cat.   am

D 문장을 읽고 알맞은 그림을 찾아 연결하세요.

01 Is it an egg?

02 Is it an umbrella?

03 Is it an iguana?

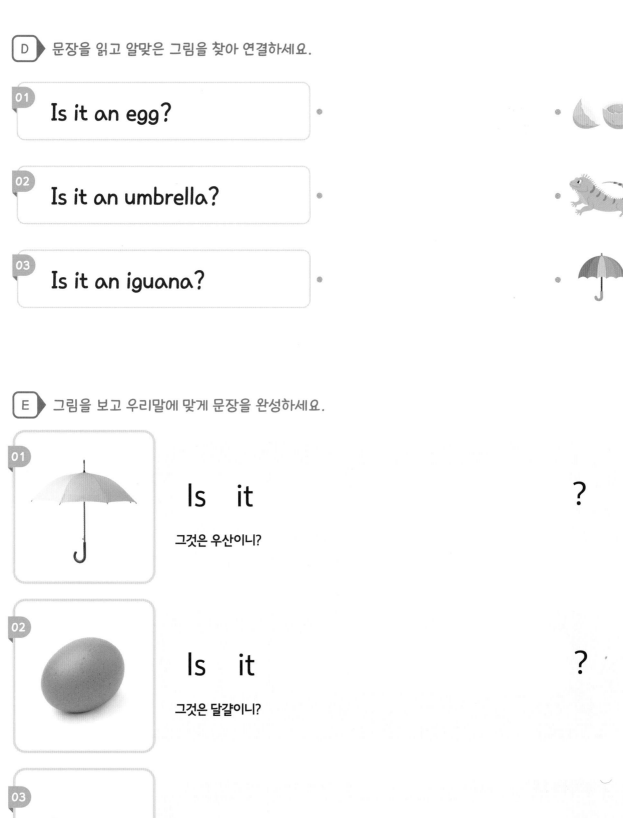

E 그림을 보고 우리말에 맞게 문장을 완성하세요.

01

Is it　　　　　?

그것은 우산이니?

02

Is it　　　　　?

그것은 달걀이니?

03

Is　　　　　?

그것은 이구아나이니?

Part 2

Unit 03

_____월 _____일

나의 평가는?
☆☆☆☆☆

Where Are You?

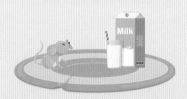

• Unit 03을 끝내고 p.82 Dictation을 하세요.

Unit 04

_____월 _____일

나의 평가는?
☆☆☆☆☆

At the Zoo

• Unit 04를 끝내고 p.83 Dictation을 하세요.
• Review를 통해 Unit 03~04를 정리하세요.

QR코드

STEP 01 기초 단어 익히기

글자, 문자	달	쥐
letter	moon	mouse
매트	우유	지도
mat	milk	map

STEP 02 기초 문장 익히기

어디에 있는지 말할 때 in을 이용해서 〈in + (the) 장소〉로 써요.

	명사	in + 명사
달에 ➡	moon	I am in the moon.
매트에 ➡	mat	I am in the mat.
우유에 ➡	milk	I am _____.

Letter m,
where are you?

Here I am.

I am in the moon.
I am in the mouse.
I am in the mat.
I am in the milk.
I am in the map.

Can you find me?

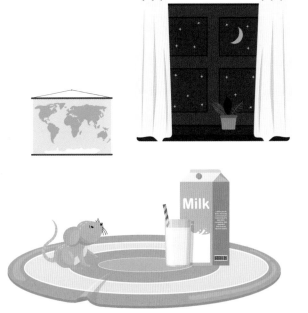

▶ **Reading Check** | 알맞은 단어를 골라 문장을 완성하세요.

It is about the _____.

a	b
m	**n**
letter m	letter n

I am in the _____.

a	b
moon	letter

▶ **Match** | 문장의 빈칸에 들어갈 알맞은 말을 연결하세요.

You can find me in the _____. •   • letter m

The _____ is in the mouse. •   • milk

영문장을 다시 읽고

Letter m,

where are you?

Here I am.

I am in the moon.

I am in the mouse.

 우리말을 확인하고

글자 m,

너는 어디에 있니?

나는 여기에 있지.

나는 달(moon)에 있어.

나는 쥐(mouse)에 있어.

 문장을 쓰며 다시 읽기

나는 매트(mat)에 있어.
나는 우유(milk)에 있어.
나는 지도(map)에 있어.
너는 날 찾을 수 있니?

 I am ___in the mat___ .

 I am ___in the milk___ .

 I am _____ .

 Can ___you find me___ ?

QR코드

STEP 01 기초 단어 익히기

얼룩말

zebra

거북이

turtle

큰

big

작은

small

빠른

fast

느린

slow

STEP 02 기초 문장 익히기

크기, 상태, 특징, 색깔 등을 나타내는 형용사는 〈am / is / are + 형용사〉로 써요.

	형용사	is + 형용사
작은 ➡	small	It is small.
빠른 ➡	fast	It is fast.
느린 ➡	slow	It _____ .

I am at the zoo.

I see an elephant.
It is big.

I see a koala.
It is small.

I see a zebra.
It is fast.

I see a turtle.
It is slow.

▶ Reading Check | 알맞은 단어를 골라 문장을 완성하세요.

_____ is at the zoo.

a	b
A cat	An elephant

I see a koala. It is _____.

a	b
big	small

▶ Match | 문장의 빈칸에 들어갈 알맞은 말을 연결하세요.

A _____ is fast.　　　•　　•　slow

A turtle is _____.　　•　　•　zebra

24

영문장을 다시 읽고

I am at the zoo.

I see an elephant.

It is big.

I see a koala.

It is small.

우리말을 확인하고

나는 동물원에 있다.

나는 코끼리를 본다.

그것은 크다.

나는 코알라를 본다.

그것은 작다.

문장을 쓰며 다시 읽기

나는 얼룩말을 본다.
그것은 빠르다.
나는 거북이를 본다.
그것은 느리다.

 I _____ see a zebra _____ .

 It _____ is fast _____ .

 I _____ .

 It _____ .

Review

A 그림을 보고 알맞은 단어를 찾아 쓰세요.

moon
mouse
mat

moon

_____

milk
map
letter

_____

zebra
turtle
big

_____

small
fast
slow

_____

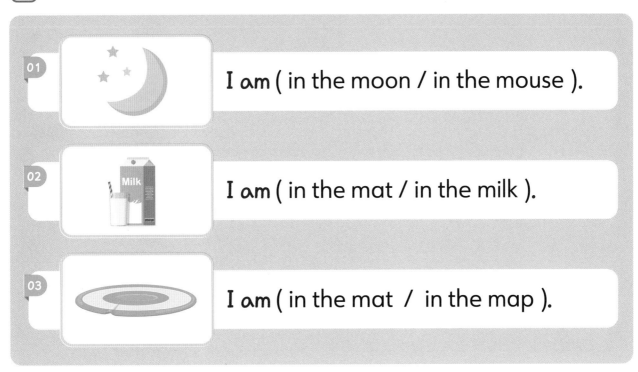

01 I am (in the moon / in the mouse).

02 I am (in the mat / in the milk).

03 I am (in the mat / in the map).

C 그림을 보고 순서에 맞게 써서 문장을 완성하세요.

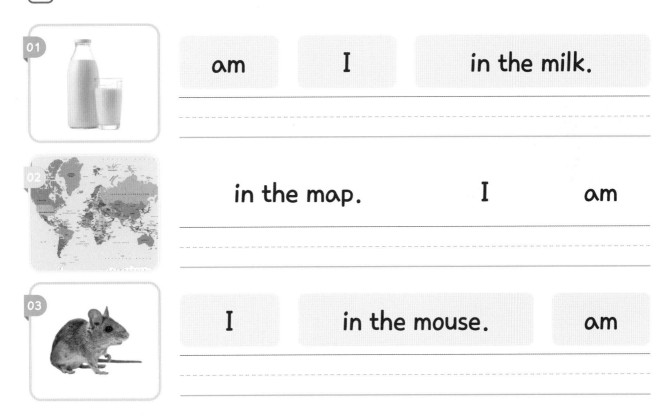

01 am   I   in the milk.

02 in the map.   I   am

03 I   in the mouse.   am

문장을 읽고 알맞은 그림을 찾아 연결하세요.

01 It is small.

02 It is big.

03 It is fast.

E 그림을 보고 우리말에 맞게 문장을 완성하세요.

01

It   is   .

그것은 느리다.

02

It   is   .

그것은 크다.

03

It   .

그것은 작다.

28

Part 3

I Like Kimbap!

QR코드

당근

carrot

오이

cucumber

주황, 주황색의

orange

초록, 초록색의

green

노랑, 노란색의

yellow

먹다

eat

사람, 사물 등이 둘 이상일 때 <명사s>로 써요.

	명사	명사s
오이	cucumber	I like cucumbers.
달걀	egg	I like eggs.
당근	carrot	I like _____ .

I like carrots.
They are orange.
I like cucumbers.
They are green.

I like eggs.
They are yellow.
I like spinach.
It is green, too.

I am ready to eat.
I like kimbap!

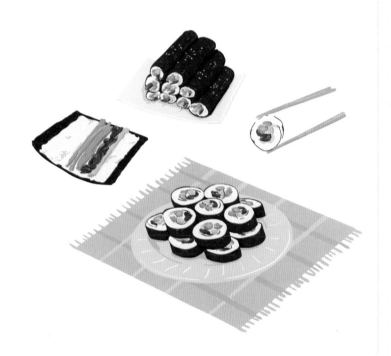

▶ **Reading Check |** 알맞은 단어를 골라 문장을 완성하세요.

It is about _____.

a	b
kimbap	cookies

_____ are orange.

a	b
Carrots	Cucumbers

▶ **Match |** 문장의 빈칸에 들어갈 알맞은 말을 연결하세요.

I like eggs. They are _____.   •   •   yellow

I like _____. They are green.   •   •   cucumbers

31

✌ 영문장을 다시 읽고

I like carrots.
They are orange.
I like cucumbers.
They are green.

✌ 우리말을 확인하고

나는 **당근들을 좋아한다.**
그것들은 주황색이다.
나는 **오이들을 좋아한다.**
그것들은 초록색이다.

✌ 문장을 쓰며 다시 읽기

나는 **달걀들을 좋아한다.**
그것들은 노란색이다.
나는 **시금치를 좋아한다.**
그것도 초록색이다.
나는 먹을 준비가 됐다.
나는 김밥을 좋아한다!

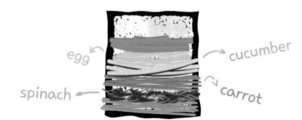

egg
cucumber
spinach
carrot

→ I _____ .

→ They _____ .

→ I like _____ spinach _____ .

→ It is _____ green _____ .

→ I am ready to _____ .

→ I like _____ kimbap _____ !

STEP 01 기초 단어 익히기

비

rain

비 오는

rainy

바람

wind

바람 부는

windy

눈

snow

눈 오는

snowy

STEP 02 기초 문장 익히기

날씨를 나타내는 단어는 〈명사 + y〉로 써요.

명사	명사 + y

비 오는 ➡ rain → It is rainy.

바람 부는 ➡ wind → It is windy.

눈 오는 ➡ snow → It is _____.

It is sunny.
You can see the sun.

It is rainy.
You can see the rain.

It is windy.
You can see the wind.

It is snowy.
You can see the snow.

What's the weather like today?

▶ **Reading Check** | 알맞은 단어를 골라 문장을 완성하세요.

It is about the _____.

color

weather

It is _____. You can see the sun.

sunny

rainy

▶ **Match** | 문장의 빈칸에 들어갈 알맞은 말을 연결하세요.

It is a _____ day. ·　　　· snow

You can see the _____. ·　　　· snowy

☝ 영문장을 다시 읽고

It is sunny.
You can see the sun.
It is rainy.
You can see the rain.

✌ 우리말을 확인하고

(날씨가) 맑다.
너는 해를 볼 수 있다.
(날씨가) 비가 온다.
너는 비를 볼 수 있다.

🖐 문장을 쓰며 다시 읽기

(날씨가) 바람이 분다.
너는 바람을 볼 수 있다.
(날씨가) 눈이 온다.
너는 눈을 볼 수 있다.
오늘 날씨는 어때?

→ It _____is windy_____ .

→ You _____can see the wind_____ .

→ It _____ .

→ You _____ .

→ What's _the weather like_ today?

A 그림을 보고 알맞은 단어를 찾아 쓰세요.

carrot
eat
cucumber

carrot _____ _____

orange
green
yellow

rain
wind
snow

rainy
windy
snowy

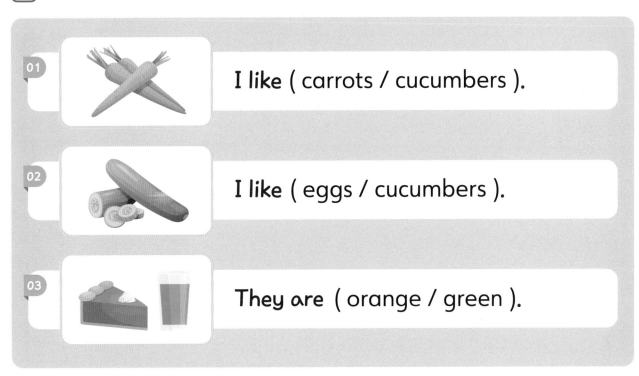

01 I like (carrots / cucumbers).

02 I like (eggs / cucumbers).

03 They are (orange / green).

C ▶ 그림을 보고 순서에 맞게 써서 문장을 완성하세요.

01 like I eggs.

02 kimbap. I like

03 They yellow. are

문장을 읽고 알맞은 그림을 찾아 연결하세요.

01 **It is snowy.**

02 **It is windy.**

03 **It is sunny.**

E 그림을 보고 우리말에 맞게 문장을 완성하세요.

01 **You   can   see   the   .**

너는 바람을 볼 수 있다.

02 **You   can   .**

너는 해를 볼 수 있다.

03 **You   .**

너는 비를 볼 수 있다.

38

Part 4

Unit 07

_____월 _____일

나의 평가는?
☆☆☆☆☆

My Messy Room

• Unit 07을 끝내고 p.86 Dictation을 하세요.

Unit 08

_____월 _____일

나의 평가는?
☆☆☆☆☆

Bears

• Unit 08을 끝내고 p.87 Dictation을 하세요.
• Review를 통해 Unit 07~08을 정리하세요.

STEP 01 기초 단어 익히기

책

book

장난감

toy

신발

shoe

양말

sock

장갑

glove

엉망

mess

STEP 02 기초 문장 익히기

짝을 이루는 명사는 항상 <명사s>로 쓰고, <There are ~>를 사용해
'~(들)이/가 있다'라고 표현할 수 있어요.

	짝을 이루는 것(명사s)	There are + 명사s
신발 ➡	shoes	There are shoes.
양말 ➡	socks	There are socks.
장갑 ➡	gloves	

There are books all over the bedroom.
There are toys all over the bedroom.
There are shoes all over the bedroom.

There are socks under the bed.
There are gloves under the bed.

My room is a mess.

Clean up your room, Ella!

Sorry, Mom. I love my messy room.

▶ **Reading Check |** 알맞은 단어를 골라 문장을 완성하세요.

It is about my messy _____.

room | hair

There are _____.

a book | gloves

▶ **Match |** 문장의 빈칸에 들어갈 알맞은 말을 연결하세요.

My room is a _____. • • mess

There are _____ under the bed. • • socks

✌ 영문장을 다시 읽고

There are books all over the bedroom.
There are toys all over the bedroom.
There are shoes all over the bedroom.

✌ 우리말을 확인하고

침실 여기저기 **책들이** 있다.

침실 여기저기 **장난감들이** 있다.

침실 여기저기 **신발들이** 있다.

✌ 문장을 쓰며 다시 읽기

침대 밑에 **양말들이** 있다.
침대 밑에 **장갑들이** 있다.
내 방은 엉망이다.
네 방을 청소해라.
나는 내 엉망인 방을 사랑한다.

→ There ___are socks___ under the bed.

→ There _____ under the bed.

→ My room is a ___mess___ .

→ ___Clean up your room___ .

→ I ___love my messy room___ .

QR코드

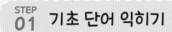

STEP 01 기초 단어 익히기

아이

child

날카로운

sharp

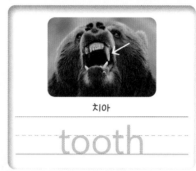

치아

tooth

발톱

claw

발

foot

거대한

huge

STEP 02 기초 문장 익히기

둘 이상을 나타낼 때 불규칙하게 변화하는 단어들을 써 봐요.

		하나	둘 이상 : 불규칙 변화
아이들	⇒	child	Children love bears.
치아(들)	⇒	tooth	They have sharp teeth.
발(들)	⇒	foot	They have sharp feet.

Children love to see bears.

They have sharp teeth.
They have sharp claws.

They have big feet.
They have huge bodies.

They sleep all winter.
They do not eat in winter.

▶ **Reading Check** | 알맞은 단어를 골라 문장을 완성하세요.

It is about _____.

a bears   b children

Bears have sharp _____.

a body   b teeth

▶ **Match** | 문장의 빈칸에 들어갈 알맞은 말을 연결하세요.

Bears have huge _____.   •   •   feet

Bears have big _____.   •   •   bodies

44

✌️ 영문장을 다시 읽고

Children love to see bears.
They have sharp teeth.
They have sharp claws.

✌️ 우리말을 확인하고

아이들은 **곰들을** 보고 싶어한다.

그것들은 날카로운 **이빨들을** 가지고 있다.

그것들은 날카로운 **발톱들을** 가지고 있다.

✌️ 문장을 쓰며 다시 읽기

그것들은 큰 **발들을** 가지고 있다.
그것들은 거대한 몸을 가지고 있다.
그것들은 겨울 내내 잔다.
그것들은 겨울에 먹지 않는다.

⇒ They _____ .

⇒ They _____ have huge bodies _____ .

⇒ They _____ sleep all winter _____ .

⇒ They _____ do not eat in winter _____ .

Review

Unit 07~08

A 그림을 보고 알맞은 단어를 찾아 쓰세요.

book

toy

mess

book _____ _____

---

shoe

sock

glove

_____ _____ _____

---

child

tooth

foot

_____ _____ _____

---

sharp

claw

huge

_____ _____ _____

그림을 보고 알맞은 단어를 찾아 동그라미 하세요.

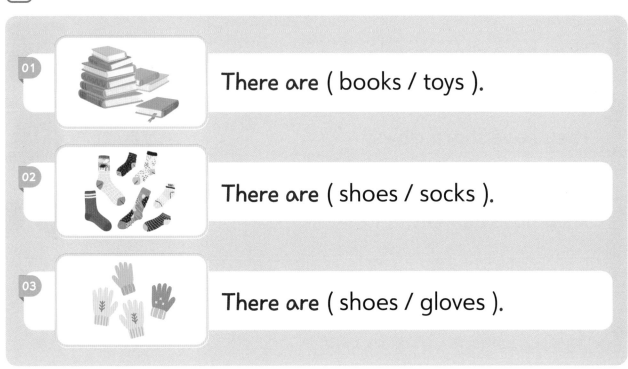

01 There are (books / toys).

02 There are (shoes / socks).

03 There are (shoes / gloves).

C 그림을 보고 순서에 맞게 써서 문장을 완성하세요.

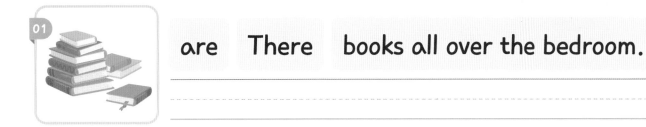

01 are　There　books all over the bedroom.

02 There　shoes all over the bedroom.　are

03 toys all over the bedroom.　are　There

47

01 They have sharp teeth. ·

·

02 They have sharp claws. ·

·

03 They have big feet. ·

·

E ▶ 그림을 보고 우리말에 맞게 문장을 완성하세요.

They   have   big   .

그것들은 큰 발들을 가지고 있다.

They   sharp   .

그것들은 날카로운 이빨들을 가지고 있다.

They   .

그것들은 날카로운 발톱들을 가지고 있다.

Part 5

Unit 09

_____월 _____일

나의 평가는?
☆ ☆ ☆ ☆ ☆

We Are Friends

• Unit 09를 끝내고 p.88 Dictation을 하세요.

Unit 10

_____월 _____일

나의 평가는?
☆ ☆ ☆ ☆ ☆

I Like You

• Unit 10을 끝내고 p.89 Dictation을 하세요.
• Review를 통해 Unit 09~10을 정리하세요.

We Are Friends

STEP 01 기초 단어 익히기

친구
friend

놀다
play

함께
together

입고(신고) 있다
wear

달리다, 뛰다
run

물웅덩이
puddle

STEP 02 기초 문장 익히기 주어와 동사의 순서에 주의해서 〈주어+동사〉로 써요.

		동사	주어 + 동사
놀다	⇒	play	We play together.
하다	⇒	do	We do things together.
달리다	⇒	run	together.

Ella and I are friends.
We wear rain boots together.
We run together in the rain.
We jump in the puddle.
We do everything together.

We love snow.
We play in the snow all day long.

"Achoo, achoo!"

Did we catch a cold?

▶ **Reading Check |** 알맞은 단어를 골라 문장을 완성하세요.

It is about a _____.

a friend	b family

We _____ together in the rain.

a run	b eat

▶ **Match |** 문장의 빈칸에 들어갈 알맞은 말을 연결하세요.

Ella and I _____ rain boots together. •   • play

We _____ in the snow. •   • wear

51

✌ 영문장을 다시 읽고

Ella and I are friends.
We wear rain boots together.
We run together in the rain.
We jump in the puddle.

✌ 우리말을 확인하고

엘라와 나는 친구이다.
우리는 같이 장화를 신고 있다.
우리는 같이 빗속에서 달린다.
우리는 물웅덩이에서 점프한다.

✌ 문장을 쓰며 다시 읽기

우리는 같이 모든 것을 한다.
우리는 눈을 사랑한다.
우리는 하루 종일 눈 속에서 논다.
에취, 에취.
우리는 감기에 걸렸나?

→ We _____do everything together_____ .

→ We _____love snow_____ .

→ _____ in the snow all day long.

→ Achoo, achoo.

→ Did _____we catch a cold_____ ?

I Like You

QR코드

STEP
01 기초 단어 익히기

스포츠(운동, 경기)
sport

축구
soccer

타다
ride

읽다
read

만화책
comic book

(똑)같은
same

STEP
02 기초 문장 익히기
주어가 'Matt(이름), He, She' 등일 때 동사는 <동사 + s>로 써요.

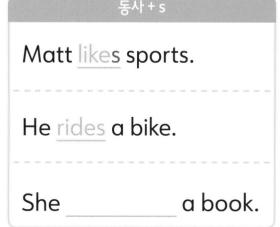

	동사	동사 + s
좋아하다	like	Matt likes sports.
타다	ride	He rides a bike.
읽다	read	She _____ a book.

I like sports.
Matt likes sports, too.
I play soccer.
Matt plays soccer, too.

I ride a bike.
Matt rides a bike, too.
I read comic books.
Matt reads comic books, too.

We do the same things.
We are best friends.

▶ **Reading Check** | 본문의 내용과 같으면 Yes, 다르면 No에 표시하세요.

| Matt and I like sports. | ☐ YES · ☐ NO |
| Matt plays tennis. | ☐ YES ☐ NO |

▶ **Match** | 그림을 보고 알맞은 문장과 연결하세요.

Matt rides a bike.

Matt and I read comic books.

영문장을 다시 읽고

I like sports.
Matt likes sports, too.
I play soccer.
Matt plays soccer, too.

우리말을 확인하고

나는 스포츠를 좋아한다.
매트도 스포츠를 좋아한다.
나는 축구를 한다.
매트도 축구를 한다.

문장을 쓰며 다시 읽기

나는 자전거를 탄다.
매트도 자전거를 탄다.
나는 만화를 읽는다.
매트도 만화를 읽는다.
우리는 같은 것을 한다.
우리는 가장 좋은 친구이다.

→ I ___ride a bike___ .

→ Matt _____ , too.

→ I ___read comic books___ .

→ Matt _____ , too.

→ We ___do the same things___ .

→ We are best _____ .

55

A 그림을 보고 알맞은 단어를 찾아 쓰세요.

play
wear
friend

play

run
puddle
together

sport
soccer
comic book

ride
read
same

그림을 보고 알맞은 단어를 찾아 동그라미 하세요.

01 We (wear / jump) in the puddle.

02 We (play / jump) in the snow.

03 We (run / wear) together in the rain.

C 그림을 보고 순서에 맞게 써서 문장을 완성하세요.

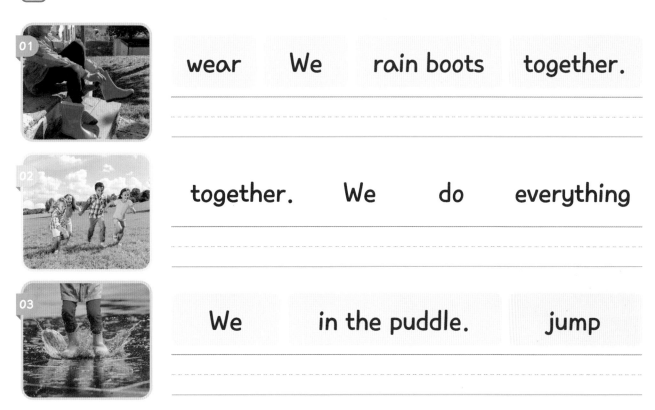

01 wear   We   rain boots   together.

02 together.   We   do   everything

03 We   in the puddle.   jump

문장을 완성하는 데 필요한 단어를 찾아 연결하세요.

01 Matt   sports, too. •

 • rides

02 Matt   soccer, too. •

 • likes

03 Matt   a bike, too. •

 • plays

E 그림을 보고 우리말에 맞게 문장을 완성하세요.

01 Matt   soccer , too .

매트도 축구를 한다.

02 Matt   , too .

매트도 운동을 좋아한다.

03 Matt   , too .

매트도 만화책을 읽는다.

Part 6

Unit 11

_____월 _____일

나의 평가는?
☆☆☆☆☆

My Little Sister

• Unit 11을 끝내고 p.90 Dictation을 하세요.

Unit 12

_____월 _____일

나의 평가는?
☆☆☆☆☆

I Do Not Like It

• Unit 12를 끝내고 p.91 Dictation을 하세요.
• Review를 통해 Unit 11~12를 정리하세요.

My Little Sister

QR코드

STEP 01 기초 단어 익히기

자매 (여동생, 언니, 누나)

sister

가지고 있다

have

울다

cry

가다

go

조심하다

watch out

하루종일

all day long

STEP 02 기초 문장 익히기   주어가 'He, She, It'등일 때 〈cry → cries, have → has, go → goes〉로 바꿔 써요.

	동사	She + 동사
울다 ➡	cry	She cries all day long.
가지고 있다 ➡	have	She has a little sister.
가다 ➡	go	up on the sofa.

I have a little sister.
What does she do all day long?

She cries all day long.
Don't cry, Ella.

She goes up on the sofa all day long.
Watch out, Ella.

She reads books all day long.
Don't eat it, Ella.

▶ Reading Check | 본문의 내용과 같으면 Yes, 다르면 No에 표시하세요.

| The story is about my toy. | ☐ YES | ☐ NO |
| My sister cries all day long. | ☐ YES | ☐ NO |

▶ Match | 그림을 보고 알맞은 문장과 연결하세요.

●　　　　　● She reads books all day long.

●　　　　　● She goes up on the sofa all day long.

영문장을 다시 읽고

I have a little sister.
What does she do all day long?
She cries all day long.
Don't cry, Ella.

 우리말을 확인하고

나는 어린 여동생이 있다.

그녀는 하루 종일 무엇을 하니?

그녀는 하루 종일 운다.

울지 마, 엘라.

 문장을 쓰며 다시 읽기

그녀는 하루 종일 소파 위로 올라간다.
조심해, 엘라.
그녀는 하루 종일 책을 읽는다.
그것을 먹지 마, 엘라.

→ She _goes up on the sofa_ all day long.

→ _Watch out_ , Ella.

→ She _____.

→ _Don't eat it_ , Ella.

아침 식사

breakfast

걷다

walk

학교

school

아이스크림

ice cream

추운

cold

버스로

by bus

주어가 'I, You, We, They'일 때 '~하지 않는다'라는 뜻의 부정 표현은 〈주어 + do not + 동사〉로 써요.

	긍정	주어 + do not + 동사
먹지 않는다	have	I do not have breakfast.
걷지 않는다	walk	I do not walk to school.
좋아하지 않는다	like	I _____ ice cream.

Mia has breakfast.
I do not have breakfast.

Mia walks to school.
I do not walk to school.
I go to school by bus.

Mia likes ice cream.
I do not like ice cream.
It is too cold for ice cream.
Achoo, achoo.

Sorry, Mia.

▶ **Reading Check** | 본문의 내용과 같으면 Yes, 다르면 No에 표시하세요.

| Mia and I don't like ice cream. | ☐ YES | ☐ NO |
| I don't go to school by bus. | ☐ YES | ☐ NO |

* do not의 줄임 표현은 don't로 써요.

▶ **Match** | 그림을 보고 알맞은 문장과 연결하세요.

I don't like ice cream.

I don't walk to school.

✌️ 영문장을 다시 읽고

Mia has breakfast.
I do not have breakfast.
Mia walks to school.
I do not walk to school.
I go to school by bus.

✌️ 우리말을 확인하고

미아는 아침을 먹는다.
나는 아침을 먹지 않는다.
미아는 학교에 걸어간다.
나는 학교에 걸어가지 않는다.
나는 버스로 학교에 간다.

✌️ 문장을 쓰며 다시 읽기

미아는 아이스크림을 좋아한다.
나는 아이스크림을 좋아하지 않는다.
아이스크림을 먹기에는 너무 춥다.
에취, 에취. 미안해, 미아야.

→ Mia ___likes ice cream___ .

→ I _____ .

→ ___It is too cold for ice cream___ .

→ Achoo, achoo. ___Sorry, Mia___ .

Review

그림을 보고 알맞은 단어를 찾아 쓰세요.

have		
cry		
go		

have

sister		
watch out		
all day long		

breakfast		
school		
ice cream		

walk		
cold		
by bus		

B   그림을 보고 알맞은 단어를 찾아 동그라미 하세요.

01   She (cry / cries) all day long.

02   She (go / goes) up on the sofa.

03   She (reads / read) books.

C   그림을 보고 순서에 맞게 써서 문장을 완성하세요.

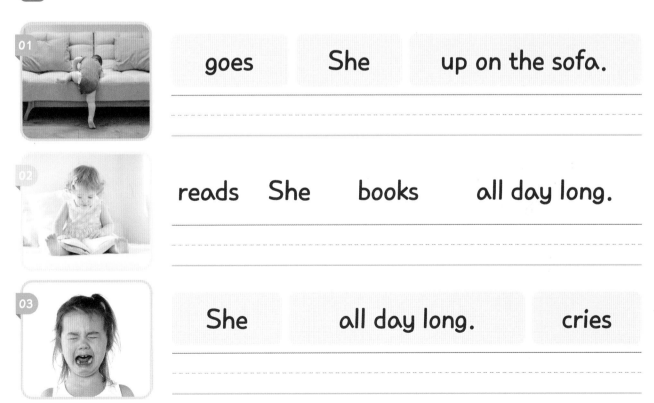

01   goes   She   up on the sofa.

02   reads   She   books   all day long.

03   She   all day long.   cries

문장을 완성하는 데 필요한 단어를 찾아 연결하세요.

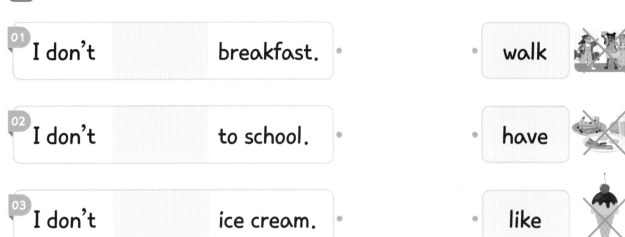

01 I don't _____ breakfast. · · walk

02 I don't _____ to school. · · have

03 I don't _____ ice cream. · · like

E 그림을 보고 우리말에 맞게 문장을 완성하세요.

01 I   don't   have   .

나는 아침을 먹지 않는다.

02 I   don't   .

나는 아이스크림을 좋아하지 않는다.

03 I   .

나는 학교에 걸어가지 않는다.

68

Part 7

Unit 13

_____월 _____일

나의 평가는?
☆☆☆☆☆

What Does He Do?

• Unit 13을 끝내고 p.92 Dictation을 하세요.

Unit 14

_____월 _____일

나의 평가는?
☆☆☆☆☆

Four Seasons

• Unit 14를 끝내고 p.93 Dictation을 하세요.
• Review를 통해 Unit 13~14를 정리하세요.

What Does He Do?

STEP 01 기초 단어 익히기

굽다

bake

일하다

work

돕다

help

가르치다

teach

키우다

grow

요리하다

cook

STEP 02 기초 문장 익히기

주어가 'He, She' 등일 때 '~하지 않는다'라는 뜻의 부정 표현은
〈주어 + does not + 동사〉로 써요.

	긍정	주어 + does not + 동사
일하지 않는다	He works	He does not work.
가르치지 않는다	She teaches	She does not teach.
요리하지 않는다	He cooks	

Mike is a baker.
He bakes bread.
He does not work at a school.

Ella is a police officer.
She helps people.
She does not teach students.

Matt is a farmer.
He grows food.
He does not cook food.

▶ **Reading Check** | 본문의 내용과 같으면 Yes, 다르면 No에 표시하세요.

Mike doesn't bake bread.	☐ YES	☐ NO
Ella helps people.	☐ YES	☐ NO

* does not의 줄임 표현은 doesn't로 써요.

▶ **Match** | 그림을 보고 알맞은 문장과 연결하세요.

She doesn't teach students.

He doesn't cook food.

✌ 영문장을 다시 읽고

Mike is a baker.

He bakes bread.

He does not work at a school.

✌ 우리말을 확인하고

마이크는 제빵사이다.

그는 빵을 굽는다.

그는 학교에서 일하지 않는다.

✌ 문장을 쓰며 다시 읽기

엘라는 경찰관이다.
그녀는 사람들을 돕는다.
그녀는 학생들을 가르치지 않는다.
매트는 농부이다.
그는 식량을 기른다.
그는 음식을 요리하지 않는다.

→ **Ella is a** _____police officer_____ .

→ **She** _____helps people_____ .

→ **She** _____does not teach students_____ .

→ **Matt is a** _____farmer_____ .

→ **He** _____grows food_____ .

→ **He** _____ .

STEP 01 기초 단어 익히기

나무	나뭇잎	봄
tree	leaf	spring
여름	변하다	가을
summer	change	fall

STEP 02 기초 문장 익히기

문장 앞에 Do를 써서 의문문을 써 봐요.

Do + 주어 + 동사 ~?

Trees grow new leaves. ➡ Do trees grow new leaves?

Trees have green leaves. ➡ Do trees have green leaves?

Trees change color. ➡ _____ color?

Do trees grow new leaves?

Yes, they do. It is spring.

Do trees have green leaves?

Yes, they do. It is summer.

Do leaves change color?

Yes, they do. It is fall.

Do trees have many leaves?

No, they don't. It is winter.

▶ **Reading Check | 알맞은 단어를 골라 문장을 완성하세요.**

It is spring. Trees grow _____.

color

new leaves

Leaves change color. It is _____.

summer

fall

▶ **Match | 문장의 빈칸에 들어갈 알맞은 말을 연결하세요.**

_____ trees have green leaves?   •   •   Do trees

_____ have many leaves?   •   •   Do

✌ 영문장을 다시 읽고

Do trees grow new leaves?
Yes, they do.
It is spring.
Do trees have green leaves?
Yes, they do.
It is summer.

✌ 우리말을 확인하고

나무들은 새 잎이 자라니?

응, 맞아.

봄이지.

나무들은 초록 잎이 있니?

응, 맞아.

여름이야.

✌ 문장을 쓰며 다시 읽기

나뭇잎들은 색이 변하니?
응, 맞아. 가을이지.
나무들은 잎이 많이 있니?
아니, 그렇지 않아. 겨울이야.

→ Do ___leaves change___ color?

→ ___Yes, they do___ . ___It is fall___ .

→ Do _____ many leaves?

→ ___No, they don't___ . ___It is winter___ .

A 그림을 보고 알맞은 단어를 찾아 쓰세요.

| bake |
| work |
| help |

bake
_____
_____

| teach |
| grow |
| cook |

_____
_____
_____

| spring |
| summer |
| fall |

_____
_____
_____

| tree |
| leaf |
| change |

_____
_____
_____

B 그림을 보고 알맞은 단어를 찾아 동그라미 하세요.

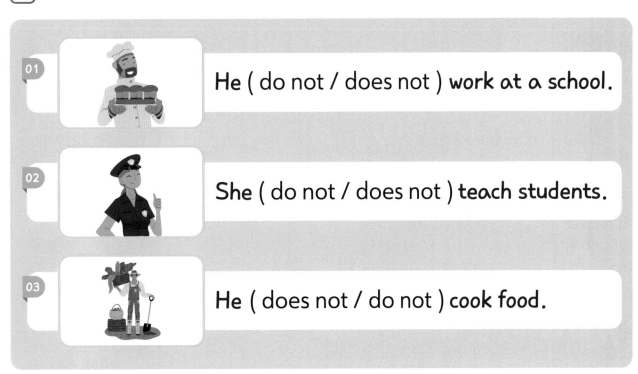

01 He (do not / does not) work at a school.

02 She (do not / does not) teach students.

03 He (does not / do not) cook food.

C 그림을 보고 순서에 맞게 써서 문장을 완성하세요.

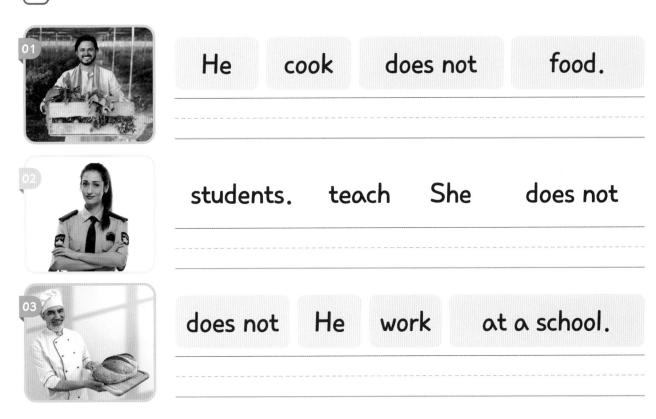

01 He   cook   does not   food.

02 students.   teach   She   does not

03 does not   He   work   at a school.

D 문장을 완성하는 데 필요한 단어를 찾아 연결하세요.

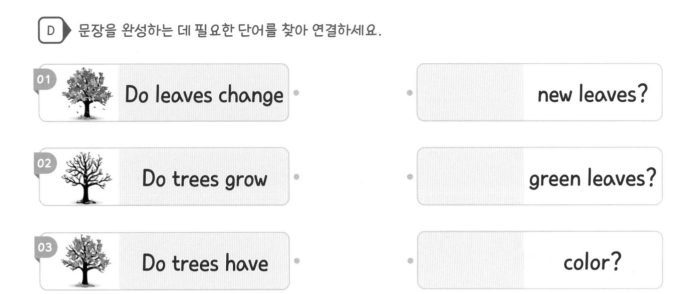

01　Do leaves change ・　　　・ new leaves?

02　Do trees grow ・　　　・ green leaves?

03　Do trees have ・　　　・ color?

E 그림을 보고 우리말에 맞게 문장을 완성하세요.

01

Do　trees　have　　　　leaves ?

나무들은 초록 잎이 있니?

02

Do　trees　　　　　　　　　　?

나무들은 새 잎이 자라니?

03

Do　leaves　　　　　　　　　　?

나뭇잎들은 색이 변하니?

Reading Starter ①

Dictation

QR코드

다음을 듣고 빈칸에 알맞은 말을 써 보세요.

Hello, Everyone

I am Moly.

I am a _____.

But today, I am a _____.

Meow, meow.

I am Matt.

I am a _____.

But today, I am a _____.

Oink, oink.

I am Ella.

I _____ a magician.

Tada!

What a surprise!

QR코드

다음을 듣고 빈칸에 알맞은 말을 써 보세요.

Happy Birthday

A : What is it?

B : Guess what is inside the _____.

A : Is it an _____?

B : No, it isn't.

A : Is it an _____?

B : No, it isn't.

A : Is it an _____?

B : No, it isn't. Open it.

A : Wow, it is a _____ dog.

B : Happy birthday. It is for you.

QR코드

다음을 듣고 빈칸에 알맞은 말을 써 보세요.

Where Are You?

Letter m,
where are you?

Here I am.

I am in the _____ .
I am in the _____ .
I am in the _____ .
I am in the _____ .
I am in the _____ .

Can you find me?

다음을 듣고 빈칸에 알맞은 말을 써 보세요.

At the Zoo

I am at the zoo.

I see an elephant.
It is _____ .

I see a koala.
It is _____ .

I see a zebra.
It is _____ .

I see a turtle.
It is _____ .

QR코드

다음을 듣고 빈칸에 알맞은 말을 써 보세요.

I Like Kimbap!

I like carrots.

They are _____.

I like cucumbers.

They are _____.

I like eggs.

They are _____.

I like spinach.

It is _____, too.

I am ready to eat.

I like kimbap!

QR코드

다음을 듣고 빈칸에 알맞은 말을 써 보세요.

The Weather

It is _____ .
You can see the sun.

It is _____ .
You can see the rain.

It is _____ .
You can see the wind.

It is _____ .
You can see the snow.

What's the weather like today?

QR코드

다음을 듣고 빈칸에 알맞은 말을 써 보세요.

My Messy Room

There are _____ all over the bedroom.
There are _____ all over the bedroom.
There are _____ all over the bedroom.

There are socks under the bed.
There _____ under the bed.

My room is a _____ .

Mom : Clean up your room, Ella!
Ella : Sorry, Mom. I love my messy room.

QR코드

다음을 듣고 빈칸에 알맞은 말을 써 보세요.

Bears

Children love to see bears.

They _____ sharp _____ .
They _____ sharp _____ .

They _____ big _____ .
They have _____ bodies.

They sleep all winter.
They do not eat in winter.

다음을 듣고 빈칸에 알맞은 말을 써 보세요.

We Are Friends

Ella and I are friends.

We _____ rain boots together.

We _____ _____ in the rain.

We _____ in the puddle.

We do everything _____ .

We love snow.

We _____ _____ the snow
all day long.

"Achoo, achoo!"

Did we catch a cold?

다음을 듣고 빈칸에 알맞은 말을 써 보세요.

I Like You

I like sports.

Matt _____, too.

I play soccer.

Matt _____, too.

I ride a bike.

Matt _____, too.

I read comic books.

Matt _____, too.

We do the _____ things.

We are best friends.

다음을 듣고 빈칸에 알맞은 말을 써 보세요.

My Little Sister

I have a little _____ .
What does she do all day long?

She _____ all day long.
Don't _____ , Ella.

She _____ up on the sofa all day long.
Watch out, Ella.

She _____ books all day long.
Don't _____ , Ella.

다음을 듣고 빈칸에 알맞은 말을 써 보세요.

I Do Not Like It

Mia _____ breakfast.

I _____ breakfast.

Mia _____ to school.

I _____ to school.

I go to school by bus.

Mia _____ ice cream.

I _____ ice cream.

It is too cold for ice cream.

Achoo, achoo.

A : Sorry, Mia.

다음을 듣고 빈칸에 알맞은 말을 써 보세요.

What Does He Do?

Mike is a baker.

He _____ bread.

He _____ at a school.

Ella is a police officer.

She _____ people.

She _____ students.

Matt is a farmer.

He _____ food.

He _____ food.

QR코드

다음을 듣고 빈칸에 알맞은 말을 써 보세요.

Four Seasons

A :   trees   new leaves?

B : Yes, they do. It is   .

A :   trees   green leaves?

B : Yes, they do. It is   .

A :   leaves   color?

B : Yes, they do. It is   .

A :   trees   many leaves?

B : No, they don't. It is   .

Reading Starter ①

정답
찾아보기

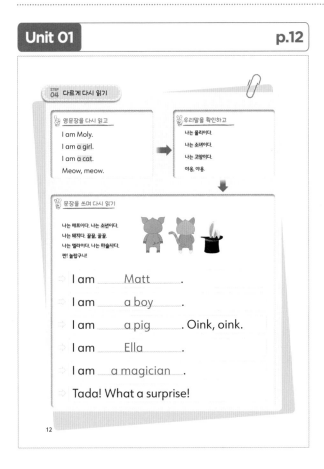

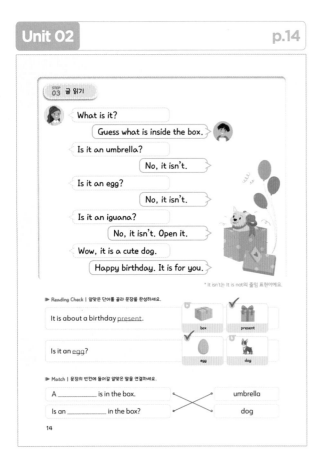

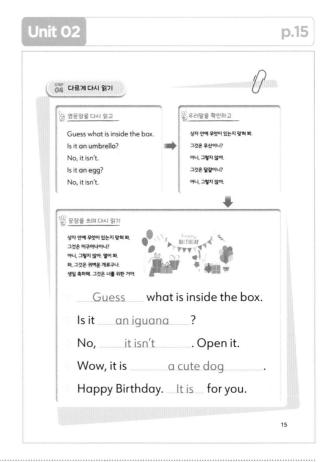

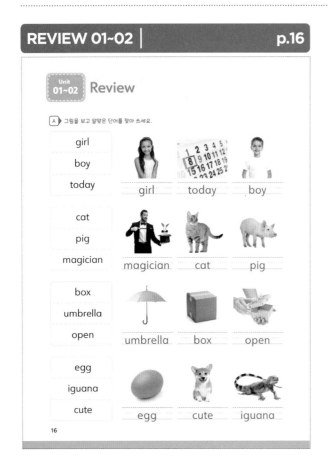

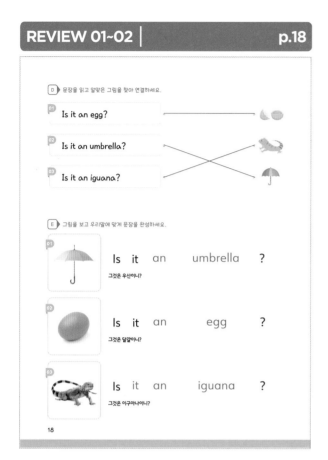

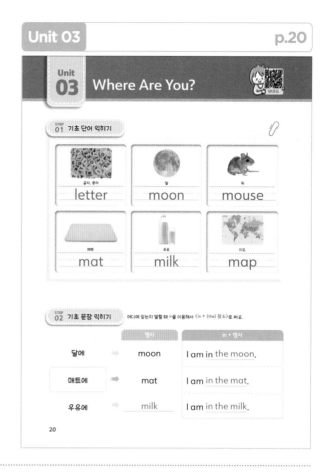

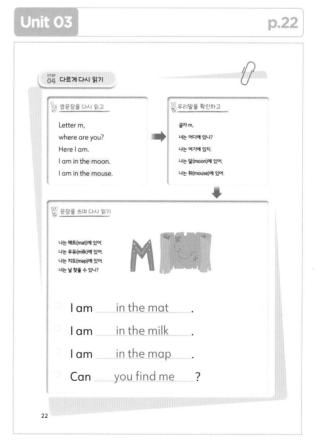

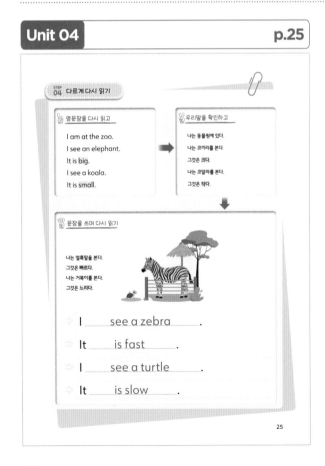

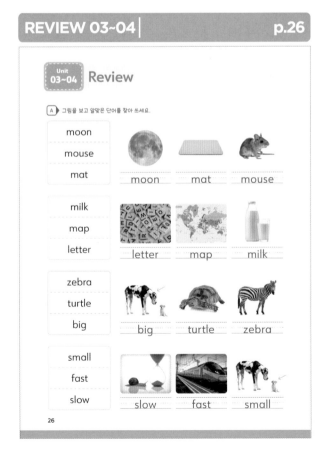

B 그림을 보고 알맞은 단어를 찾아 동그라미 하세요.

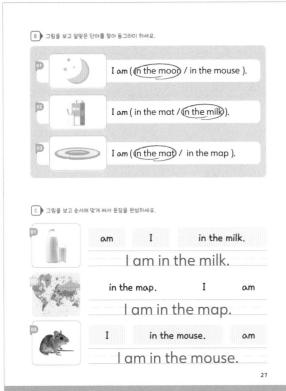

01 I am (in the moon / in the mouse).

02 I am (in the mat / in the milk).

03 I am (in the mat / in the map).

C 그림을 보고 순서에 맞게 써서 문장을 완성하세요.

01 | am | I | | in the milk.

I am in the milk.

02 in the map. | I | am

I am in the map.

03 I | in the mouse. | am

I am in the mouse.

27

D 문장을 읽고 알맞은 그림을 찾아 연결하세요.

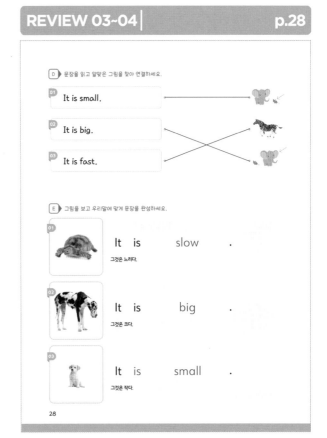

01 It is small.

02 It is big.

03 It is fast.

E 그림을 보고 우리말에 맞게 문장을 완성하세요.

01 It is slow .
그것은 느리다.

02 It is big .
그것은 크다.

03 It is small .
그것은 작다.

28

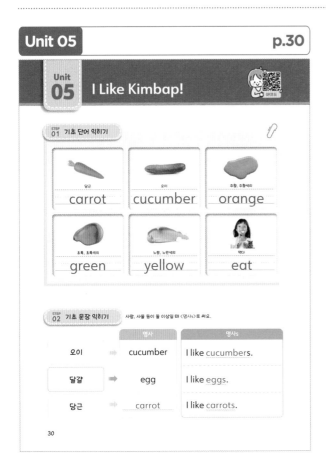

Unit 05 I Like Kimbap!

STEP 01 기초 단어 익히기

| 당근 | 오이 | 주황, 주황색의 |
| carrot | cucumber | orange |

| 초록, 초록색의 | 노랑, 노란색의 | 먹다 |
| green | yellow | eat |

STEP 02 기초 문장 익히기   사람, 사물 등이 둘 이상일 때 <명사s>로 써요.

	명사	명사s
오이	cucumber	I like cucumbers.
달걀	egg	I like eggs.
당근	carrot	I like carrots.

30

STEP 03 글 읽기

I like carrots.
They are orange.
I like cucumbers.
They are green.

I like eggs.
They are yellow.
I like spinach.
It is green, too.

I am ready to eat.
I like kimbap!

▶ Reading Check 알맞은 단어를 골라 문장을 완성하세요.

It is about kimbap.   ✓ kimbap cookies

Carrots are orange.   ✓ Carrots Cucumbers

▶ Match 문장의 빈칸에 들어갈 알맞은 말을 연결하세요.

I like eggs. They are _____.   yellow

I like _____. They are green.   cucumbers

31

99

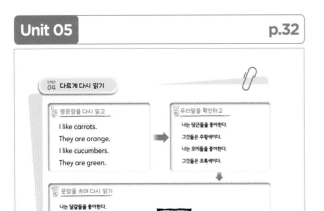

STEP 04 다르게 다시 읽기

영문장을 다시 읽고
I like carrots.
They are orange.
I like cucumbers.
They are green.

우리말을 확인하고
나는 당근들을 좋아한다.
그것들은 주황색이다.
나는 오이들을 좋아한다.
그것들은 초록색이다.

문장을 쓰며 다시 읽기
나는 달걀들을 좋아한다.
그것들은 노란색이다.
나는 시금치를 좋아한다.
그것도 초록색이다.
나는 먹을 준비가 됐다.
나는 김밥을 좋아한다!

spinach   cucumber   carrot

→ I ___like eggs___ .

→ They ___are yellow___ .

→ I like ___spinach___ .

→ It is ___green___ .

→ I am ready to ___eat___ .

→ I like ___kimbap___ !

32

Unit 06   The Weather

STEP 01 기초 단어 익히기

비	비 오는	바람
rain	rainy	wind
바람 부는	눈	눈 오는
windy	snow	snowy

STEP 02 기초 문장 익히기   날씨를 나타내는 단어는 〈명사 + y〉로 써요.

	명사	명사 + y
비 오는 →	rain	It is rainy.
바람 부는 →	wind	It is windy.
눈 오는 →	snow	It is snowy.

33

STEP 03 글 읽기

It is sunny.
You can see the sun.

It is rainy.
You can see the rain.

It is windy.
You can see the wind.

It is snowy.
You can see the snow.

What's the weather like today?

▶ Reading Check | 알맞은 단어를 골라 문장을 완성하세요.

It is about the weather.

color   weather ✓

It is sunny. You can see the sun.

sunny ✓   rainy

▶ Match | 문장의 빈칸에 들어갈 알맞은 말을 연결하세요.

It is a _____ day.   snow

You can see the _____.   snowy

34

STEP 04 다르게 다시 읽기

영문장을 다시 읽고
It is sunny.
You can see the sun.
It is rainy.
You can see the rain.

우리말을 확인하고
(날씨가) 맑다.
너는 해를 볼 수 있다.
(날씨가) 비가 온다.
너는 비를 볼 수 있다.

문장을 쓰며 다시 읽기
(날씨가) 바람이 분다.
너는 바람을 볼 수 있다.
(날씨가) 눈이 온다.
너는 눈을 볼 수 있다.
오늘 날씨는 어때?

→ It ___is windy___ .

→ You ___can see the wind___ .

→ It ___is snowy___ .

→ You ___can see the snow___ .

→ What's ___the weather like___ today?

35

100

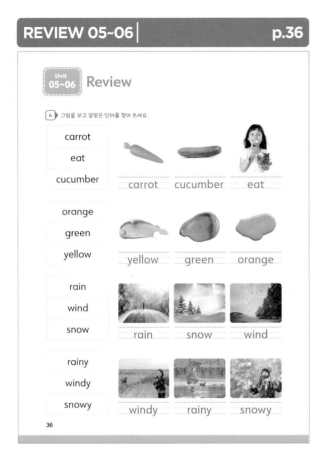

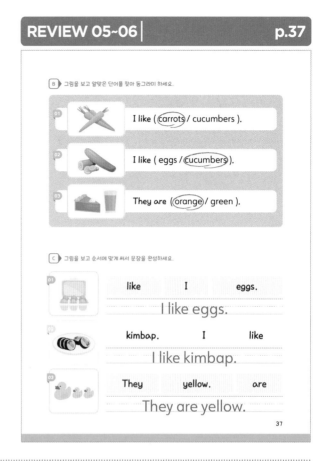

STEP 03 글 읽기

There are books all over the bedroom.
There are toys all over the bedroom.
There are shoes all over the bedroom.

There are socks under the bed.
There are gloves under the bed.

My room is a mess.

Clean up your room, Ella!

Sorry, Mom. I love my messy room.

▶ Reading Check | 알맞은 단어를 골라 문장을 완성하세요.

It is about my messy room.

room / hair

There are gloves.

a book / gloves

▶ Match | 문장의 빈칸에 들어갈 알맞은 말을 연결하세요.

My room is a _____. ——— mess
There are _____ under the bed. ——— socks

41

STEP 04 다르게 다시 읽기

영문장을 다시 읽고

There are books all over the bedroom.
There are toys all over the bedroom.
There are shoes all over the bedroom.

우리말을 확인하고

침실 여기저기 책들이 있다.
침실 여기저기 장난감들이 있다.
침실 여기저기 신발들이 있다.

문장을 쓰며 다시 읽기

침대 밑에 양말들이 있다.
침대 밑에 장갑들이 있다.
내 방은 엉망이다.
네 방을 청소해라.
나는 내 엉망인 방을 사랑한다.

> There ___are socks___ under the bed.
> There ___are gloves___ under the bed.
> My room is a ___mess___.
> ___Clean up your room___.
> I ___love my messy room___.

42

Unit 08 Bears

STEP 01 기초 단어 익히기

| 아이 | 날카로운 | 치아 |
| child | sharp | tooth |

| 발톱 | 발 | 거대한 |
| claw | foot | huge |

STEP 02 기초 문장 익히기　둘 이상을 나타낼 때 불규칙하게 변화하는 단어들을 써 봐요.

	하나	둘 이상 : 불규칙 변화
아이들	⇒ child	children love bears.
치아(들)	⇒ tooth	They have sharp teeth.
발(들)	⇒ foot	They have sharp feet.

43

STEP 03 글 읽기

Children love to see bears.

They have sharp teeth.
They have sharp claws.

They have big feet.
They have huge bodies.

They sleep all winter.
They do not eat in winter.

▶ Reading Check | 알맞은 단어를 골라 문장을 완성하세요.

It is about bears.

bears / children

Bears have sharp teeth.

body / teeth

▶ Match | 문장의 빈칸에 들어갈 알맞은 말을 연결하세요.

Bears have huge _____. ——— feet
Bears have big _____. ——— bodies

44

102

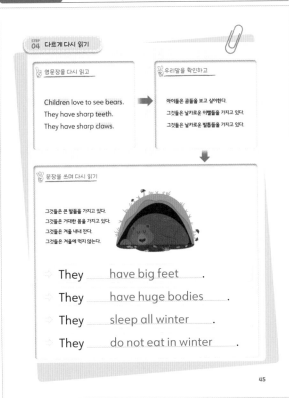

STEP 04 다르게 다시 읽기

명문장을 다시 읽고

Children love to see bears.
They have sharp teeth.
They have sharp claws.

우리말을 확인하고

아이들은 곰을 보고 싶어한다.
그것들은 날카로운 이빨들을 가지고 있다.
그것들은 날카로운 발톱들을 가지고 있다.

문장을 쓰며 다시 읽기

그것들은 큰 발들을 가지고 있다.
그것들은 거대한 몸을 가지고 있다.
그것들은 겨울 내내 잔다.
그것들은 겨울에 먹지 않는다.

They ___ have big feet ___.
They ___ have huge bodies ___.
They ___ sleep all winter ___.
They ___ do not eat in winter ___.

45

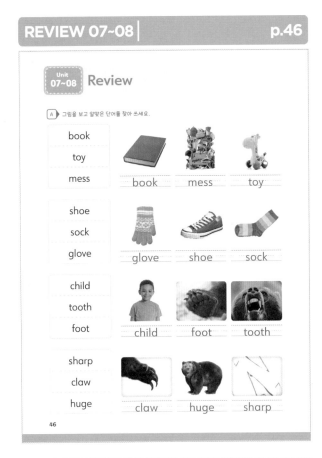

Unit 07~08 Review

A 그림을 보고 알맞은 단어를 찾아 쓰세요.

book
toy
mess

book   mess   toy

shoe
sock
glove

glove   shoe   sock

child
tooth
foot

child   foot   tooth

sharp
claw
huge

claw   huge   sharp

46

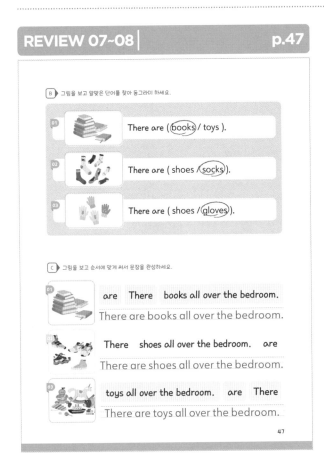

B 그림을 보고 알맞은 단어를 찾아 동그라미 하세요.

01 There are ((books) / toys).

02 There are (shoes / (socks)).

03 There are (shoes / (gloves)).

C 그림을 보고 순서에 맞게 써서 문장을 완성하세요.

01 are   There   books all over the bedroom.
There are books all over the bedroom.

02 There   shoes all over the bedroom.   are
There are shoes all over the bedroom.

03 toys all over the bedroom.   are   There
There are toys all over the bedroom.

47

D 문장을 읽고 알맞은 그림을 찾아 연결하세요.

01 They have sharp teeth.

02 They have sharp claws.

03 They have big feet.

E 그림을 보고 우리말에 맞게 문장을 완성하세요.

01 They have big feet .
그것들은 큰 발들을 가지고 있다.

02 They have sharp teeth .
그것들은 날카로운 이빨들을 가지고 있다.

03 They have sharp claws .
그것들은 날카로운 발톱들을 가지고 있다.

48

103

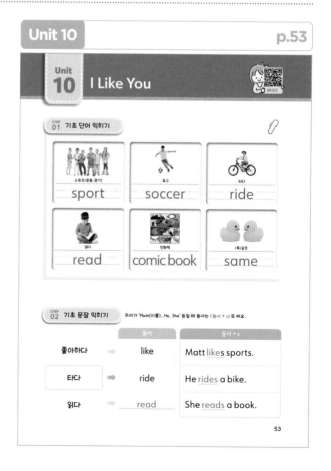

STEP 03 글 읽기

I like sports.
Matt likes sports, too.
I play soccer.
Matt plays soccer, too.

I ride a bike.
Matt rides a bike, too.
I read comic books.
Matt reads comic books, too.

We do the same things.
We are best friends.

▶ Reading Check | 본문의 내용과 같으면 Yes, 다르면 No에 표시하세요.

| Matt and I like sports. | ☑ YES ☐ NO |
| Matt plays tennis. | ☐ YES ☑ NO |

▶ Match | 그림을 보고 알맞은 문장과 연결하세요.

Matt rides a bike.

Matt and I read comic books.

54

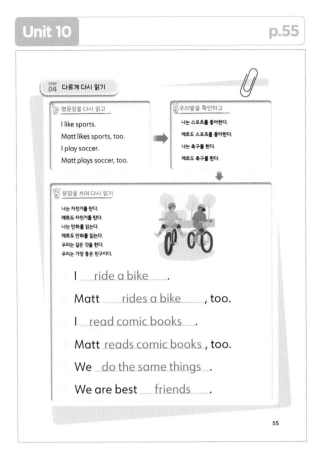

STEP 04 다르게 다시 읽기

영문장을 다시 읽고

I like sports.
Matt likes sports, too.
I play soccer.
Matt plays soccer, too.

우리말을 확인하고

나는 스포츠를 좋아한다.
매트도 스포츠를 좋아한다.
나는 축구를 한다.
매트도 축구를 한다.

문장을 쓰며 다시 읽기

나는 자전거를 탄다.
매트도 자전거를 탄다.
나는 만화를 읽는다.
매트도 만화를 읽는다.
우리는 같은 것을 한다.
우리는 가장 좋은 친구이다.

I ___ride a bike___ .
Matt ___rides a bike___ , too.
I ___read comic books___ .
Matt ___reads comic books___ , too.
We ___do the same things___ .
We are best ___friends___ .

55

Unit 09~10 Review

A 그림을 보고 알맞은 단어를 찾아 쓰세요.

play			
wear			
friend	play	friend	wear

run			
puddle			
together	puddle	together	run

sport			
soccer			
comic book	sport	soccer	comic book

ride			
read			
same	read	same	ride

56

B 그림을 보고 알맞은 단어를 찾아 동그라미 하세요.

01   We (wear /(jump)) in the puddle.

02   We ((play)/ jump) in the snow.

03   We ((run)/ wear) together in the rain.

C 그림을 보고 순서에 맞게 써서 문장을 완성하세요.

01   wear   We   rain boots   together.
We wear rain boots together.

02   together.   We   do   everything
We do everything together.

03   We   in the puddle.   jump
We jump in the puddle.

57

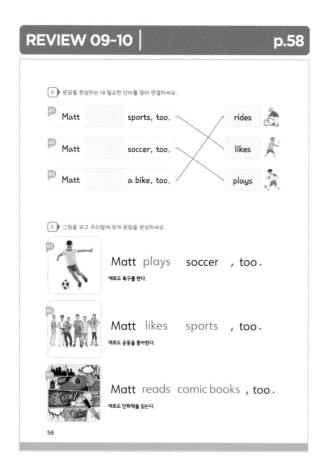

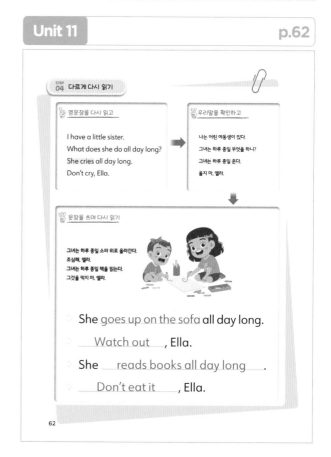

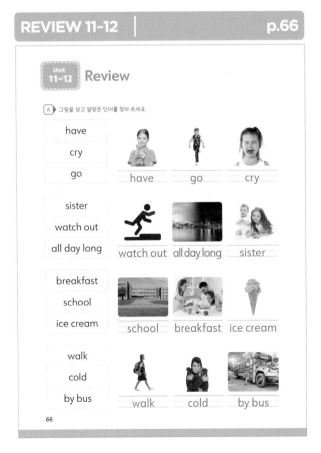

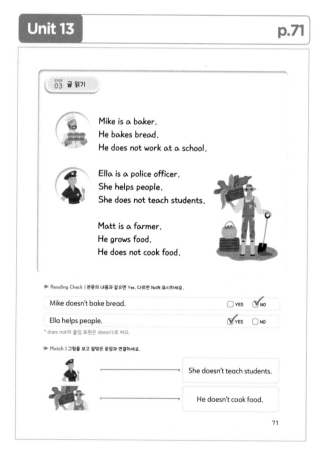

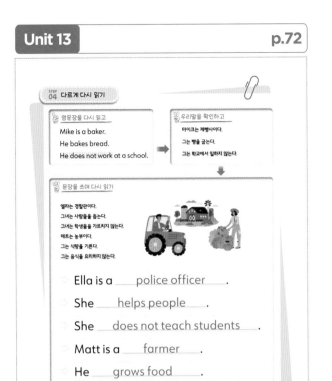

STEP 04 다르게 다시 읽기

🖐 영문장을 다시 읽고
Mike is a baker.
He bakes bread.
He does not work at a school.

🖐 우리말을 확인하고
마이크는 제빵사이다.
그는 빵을 굽는다.
그는 학교에서 일하지 않는다.

🖐 문장을 쓰며 다시 읽기
엘라는 경찰관이다.
그녀는 사람들을 돕는다.
그녀는 학생들을 가르치지 않는다.
매트는 농부이다.
그는 식량을 기른다.
그는 음식을 요리하지 않는다.

Ella is a ___police officer___.
She ___helps people___.
She ___does not teach students___.
Matt is a ___farmer___.
He ___grows food___.
He ___does not cook food___.

72

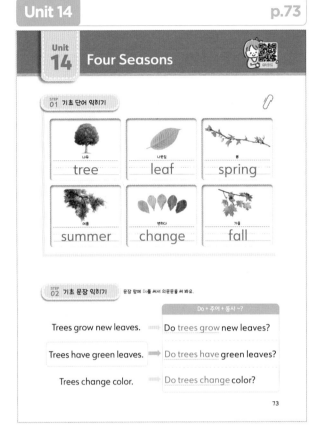

Unit 14 Four Seasons

STEP 01 기초 단어 익히기

| tree | leaf | spring |
| summer | change | fall |

나무 / 나뭇잎 / 봄 / 여름 / 변하다 / 가을

STEP 02 기초 문장 익히기   문장 앞에 Do를 써서 의문문을 써 봐요.

Do + 주어 + 동사 ~?

Trees grow new leaves. ➡ Do trees grow new leaves?

Trees have green leaves. ➡ Do trees have green leaves?

Trees change color. ➡ Do trees change color?

73

STEP 03 글 읽기

Do trees grow new leaves?
Yes, they do. It is spring.
Do trees have green leaves?
Yes, they do. It is summer.
Do leaves change color?
Yes, they do. It is fall.
Do trees have many leaves?
No, they don't. It is winter.

▶ Reading Check | 알맞은 단어를 골라 문장을 완성하세요.

It is spring. Trees grow _new leaves_.

color / new leaves ✓

Leaves change color. It is _fall_.

summer / fall

▶ Match | 문장의 빈칸에 들어갈 알맞은 말을 연결하세요.

_____ trees have green leaves?   Do trees

_____ have many leaves?   Do

74

STEP 04 다르게 다시 읽기

🖐 영문장을 다시 읽고
Do trees grow new leaves?
Yes, they do.
It is spring.
Do trees have green leaves?
Yes, they do.
It is summer.

🖐 우리말을 확인하고
나무들은 새 잎이 자라니?
응, 맞아.
봄이지.
나무들은 초록 잎이 있니?
응, 맞아.
여름이야.

🖐 문장을 쓰며 다시 읽기
나뭇잎들은 색이 변하니?
응, 맞아. 가을이지.
나무들은 잎이 많이 있니?
아니, 그렇지 않아. 겨울이야.

Do ___leaves change___ color?
___Yes, they do___. ___It is fall___.
Do ___trees have___ many leaves?
___No, they don't___. ___It is winter___.

75

109

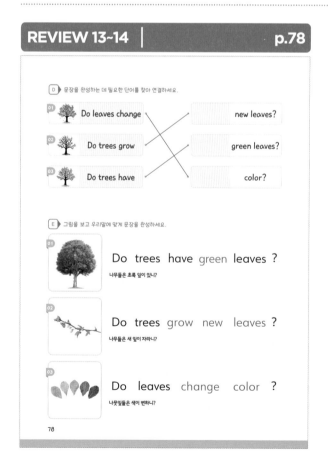

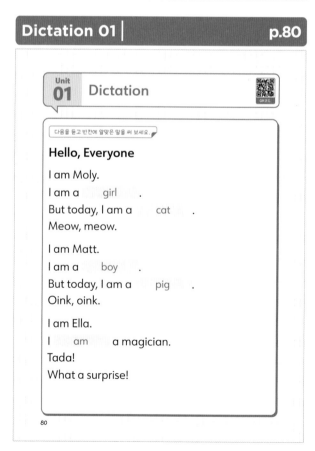

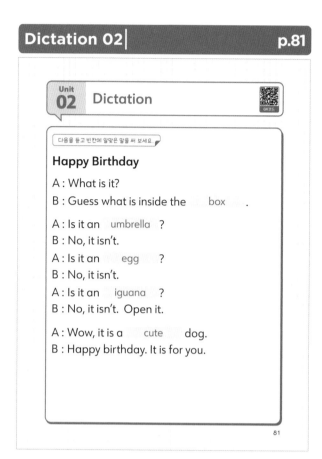

Happy Birthday

A : What is it?

B : Guess what is inside the　box　.

A : Is it an　umbrella　?

B : No, it isn't.

A : Is it an　egg　?

B : No, it isn't.

A : Is it an　iguana　?

B : No, it isn't. Open it.

A : Wow, it is a　cute　dog.

B : Happy birthday. It is for you.

81

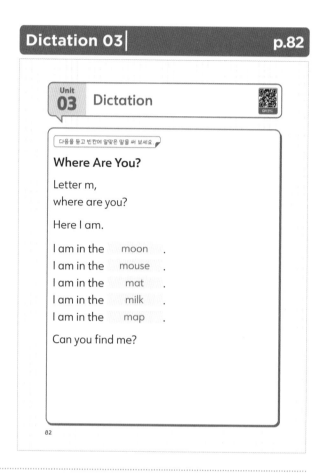

Where Are You?

Letter m,

where are you?

Here I am.

I am in the　moon　.

I am in the　mouse　.

I am in the　mat　.

I am in the　milk　.

I am in the　map　.

Can you find me?

82

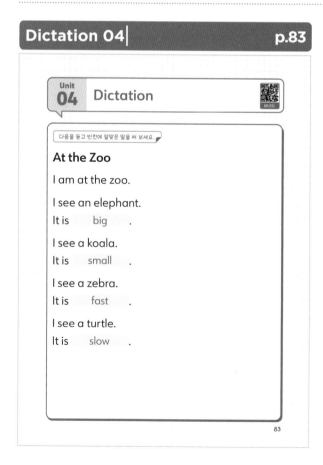

At the Zoo

I am at the zoo.

I see an elephant.

It is　big　.

I see a koala.

It is　small　.

I see a zebra.

It is　fast　.

I see a turtle.

It is　slow　.

83

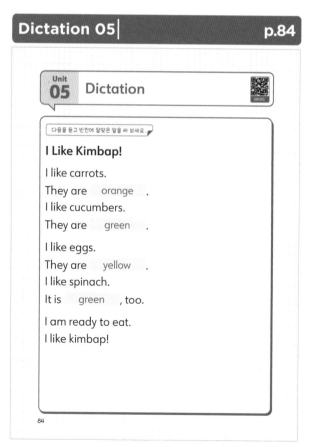

I Like Kimbap!

I like carrots.

They are　orange　.

I like cucumbers.

They are　green　.

I like eggs.

They are　yellow　.

I like spinach.

It is　green　, too.

I am ready to eat.

I like kimbap!

84

111

다음을 듣고 빈칸에 알맞은 말을 써 보세요.

The Weather

It is _sunny_ .
You can see the sun.

It is _rainy_ .
You can see the rain.

It is _windy_ .
You can see the wind.

It is _snowy_ .
You can see the snow.

What's the weather like today?

85

다음을 듣고 빈칸에 알맞은 말을 써 보세요.

My Messy Room

There are _books_ all over the bedroom.
There are _toys_ all over the bedroom.
There are _shoes_ all over the bedroom.

There are socks under the bed.
There _are_ _gloves_ under the bed.

My room is a _mess_ .

Mom : Clean up your room, Ella!
Ella : Sorry, Mom. I love my messy room.

86

다음을 듣고 빈칸에 알맞은 말을 써 보세요.

Bears

Children love to see bears.

They _have_ sharp _teeth_ .
They _have_ sharp _claws_ .

They _have_ big _feet_ .
They have _huge_ bodies.

They sleep all winter.
They do not eat in winter.

87

다음을 듣고 빈칸에 알맞은 말을 써 보세요.

We Are Friends

Ella and I are friends.
We _wear_ rain boots together.
We _run_ _together_ in the rain.

We _jump_ in the puddle.
We do everything _together_ .

We love snow.
We _play_ _in_ the snow
all day long.

"Achoo, achoo!"

Did we catch a cold?

88

112

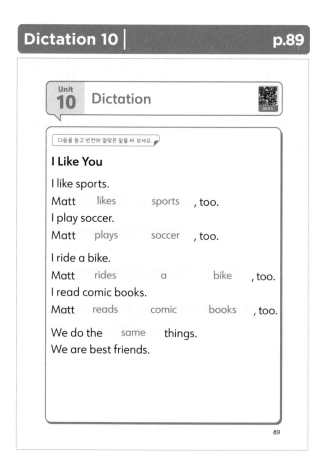

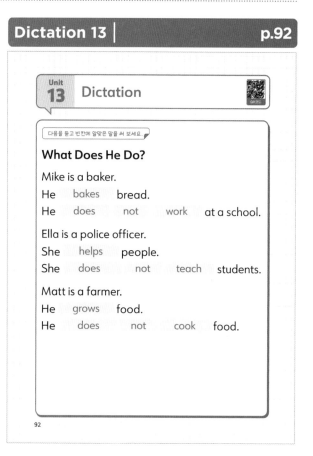

Unit 14 Dictation

다음을 듣고 빈칸에 알맞은 말을 써 보세요.

Four Seasons

A :   Do   trees   grow   new leaves?
B : Yes, they do. It is   spring   .

A :   Do   trees   have   green leaves?
B : Yes, they do. It is   summer   .

A :   Do   leaves   change   color?
B : Yes, they do. It is   fall   .

A :   Do   trees   have   many leaves?
B : No, they don't. It is   winter   .

93

'공부 습관'이야말로 가장 큰 재능입니다.
재능많은영어연구소는 최고의 학습 효과를 내는
최적의 학습 플랜을 고민합니다.

소장 윤미영

경희대학교 영문학과와 같은 대학에서 석사학위를 받았습니다. 20여 년 동안 지학사, 디딤돌, 키 영어학습방법연구소, 롱테일 교육연구소에서 초등생과 중고생을 위한 영어 교재를 기획하고 만드는 일을 해 왔습니다. 베스트셀러인《문법이 쓰기다》,《단어가 읽기다》,《구문이 독해다》, 혼공 시리즈《혼공 초등 영단어》, 《혼공 초등 영문법》, 바빠시리즈의《바빠 초등 필수 영단어》등을 집필했습니다.

초등영어 읽기독립 리딩 스타터 1

1판 1쇄 발행일 2024년 5월 13일

지은이 재능많은영어연구소

발행인 김학원
발행처 휴먼어린이
출판등록 제313-2006-000161호(2006년 7월 31일)
주소 (03991) 서울시 마포구 동교로23길 76(연남동)
전화 02-335-4422 **팩스** 02-334-3427
저자·독자 서비스 humanist@humanistbooks.com
홈페이지 www.humanistbooks.com
유튜브 youtube.com/user/humanistma **포스트** post.naver.com/hmcv
페이스북 facebook.com/hmcv2001 **인스타그램** @human_kids

편집주간 황서현 **편집** 김혜정 **원어민 검토** Sherwood Choe
표지 디자인 유주현 **본문 디자인** PRISM C **음원 제작** 109Sound
용지 화인페이퍼 **인쇄** 삼조인쇄 **제본** 해피문화사

ⓒ 재능많은영어연구소·윤미영, 2024

ISBN 978-89-6591-580-5 64740
ISBN 978-89-6591-576-8 64740(세트)

- 이 책은 저작권법에 따라 보호받는 저작물이므로 무단 전재와 무단 복제를 금합니다.
- 이 책의 전부 또는 일부를 이용하려면 반드시 저작권자와 휴먼어린이 출판사의 동의를 받아야 합니다.
- 사용 연령 6세 이상 종이에 베이거나 긁히지 않도록 조심하세요. 책 모서리가 날카로우니 던지거나 떨어뜨리지 마세요.